Fun *with* Panels

Create One-of-a-Kind Quilts • Tips & Techniques for Success

Cyndi McChesney

C&T PUBLISHING
Another Maker Inspired!

Text copyright © 2022 by Cynthia Ann McChesney

Photography and artwork copyright © 2022
by C&T Publishing, Inc.

Publisher: Amy Barrett-Daffin

Creative Director: Gailen Runge

Senior Editor: Roxane Cerda

Editor: Liz Aneloski

Technical Editor: Helen Frost

Cover/Book Designer: April Mostek

Production Coordinator: Tim Manibusan

Illustrator: Mary E. Flynn

Photography Assistant: Gabriel Martinez

Photography by Lauren Herberg, unless otherwise noted

Published by C&T Publishing, Inc., P.O. Box 1456, Lafayette, CA 94549

Library of Congress Cataloging-in-Publication Data

Names: McChesney, Cyndi, 1955- author.

Title: Fun with panels : create one-of-a-kind quilts, tips & techniques for success / Cyndi McChesney.

Description: Lafayette, CA : C&T Publishing, [2022] | Summary: "Fun with Panels, is a process-focused book introducing quilters to three different types of panels (solo image, multiple image and multi-frame) and how to work with each panel type. Learn design concepts that focus on creating a unified and interesting project with samples of panel quilts"-- Provided by publisher.

Identifiers: LCCN 2022021385 | ISBN 9781644032930 (trade paperback) | ISBN 9781644032947 (ebook)

Subjects: LCSH: Quilting--Patterns. | Patchwork--Patterns.

Classification: LCC TT835 .M237 2022 | DDC 746.46/041--dc23/eng/20220609

LC record available at https://lccn.loc.gov/2022021385

Printed in the USA

10 9 8 7 6 5 4 3

Dedication

For the many quilters who have participated in my workshops and asked endless questions about working with panels—this book would not exist without your curiosity and your support! And to my dear friend, Alex Anderson, for encouraging me to follow this theme and develop my unique approach to working with panels. Thank you for always encouraging me!

Acknowledgments

There are so many great panels available these days, and throughout the book, you will note a wide variety of fabric manufacturers represented. I use June Tailor 12″ × 12″ graph paper to map my projects. My go-to supplies include Aurifil 50/2 thread for piecing, Quilter's Dream battings, Signature 40-weight cotton quilting thread for the quilting. All of my quilts are designed, constructed, and quilted by me. I enjoy the entire process from start to finish.

Contents

Introduction   6

Chapter 1
Discover the Different Types of Panels   7

Chapter 2
Begin with the End in Mind   14

Chapter 3
Finding Design Inspiration   15

Chapter 4
Dealing with "Wonky" Panels and Odd-Sized Sections   23

Chapter 5
Discover the Magic in Traditional Quilt Blocks   27

Chapter 6
Working from a Map or Grid   38

Chapter 7
Gallery of Quilts   44

Chapter 8
Helpful Resources   62

About the Author   63

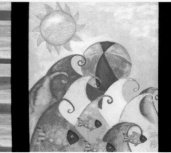

Introduction

Pre-printed panels! We love them, we buy them, and then what? Take a good look at your fabric stash and chances are that there are at least one or two of these promising gems hiding somewhere in those stacks!

The beauty of panels is the color, the design, and yes, even the possibilities. But, where do we begin? We often get home with our newly purchased panel and all the coordinating fabrics and that's the last we see of them—another purchase lost in the caverns of our stash. Because so many of my students have come to me with these very questions, I began to explore and play in an attempt to come up with some creative solutions.

I'm here to encourage you to dig those panels and fabrics out of the closet, grab some colored pencils, some scratch paper, some graph paper, and settle in for inspiration and fun!

We will walk through the steps of how to work with a variety of panels to create one-of-a-kind quilts and other special projects. You don't need a pattern—you'll learn how to create your own! But, having some basic skills is a must when working with panels.

Chapter 1

Discover the Different Types of Panels

Go take a look—how many panels have you collected and rediscovered in that fabric stash of yours? Grab one and let's get creative!

Types of Panels

Panels fall into one of 3 categories. You'll discover that all 3 styles offer endless opportunities to design unique projects.

SOLO PANELS

There are the big solo panels—one big picture if you will. These make fascinating central designs in medallion style quilts! Check out *Hummingbird Garden* (page 50) in the Gallery of Quilts.

I prefer to treat these as central medallions and create a series of borders around them, much like a traditional medallion quilt, but I don't mean simple, plain, fabric borders. Find design ideas within the panel and use them as inspiration to design your borders.

The beautiful solo panels can inspire you to create a series of "theme" borders that highlight some of the motifs from within the panel itself. In the panel at right, some themes that jump out immediately are piano keys (look at all those stripes in the sweaters!), hearts, snowflakes, and triangles (also in the patterns of the sweaters). Look for patterns or quilt block units and create borders highlighting what you see.

Arctic Wonderland by Hello Angel for Wilmington Prints

Family!, 40˝ × 49˝, by the author, 2021

Fun with Panels

Shore Thing by Blank Quilting.; see the completed quilt (page 40).

PANELS WITH MULTIPLE SIMILAR-SIZED FRAMES

This next group usually has a variety of scenes—maybe there are 12 different kittens or zoo animals on the panel.

These panels offer great options for creating a variety of projects. Remember that just because it's fabric and it's a pre-printed panel with a variety of coordinating fabrics, does not mean the end result has to be a quilt. Your panel may lend itself well to creating Halloween goodie bags for your grandchildren to carry while trick or treating, or holiday placemats for a family gathering, or tote bags for your sewing friends. You might try designing a row-by-row quilt using this type of panel. Step out of your box and dive into the deep end with me!

PANELS WITH MULTIPLE FRAMES IN A VARIETY OF SIZES

Finally, my favorite category of panels is the one with multiple frames, lots of scenes, and a wide variety of sizes. I love these panels because they offer me the greatest opportunity for variety within my designs, but each style has unique challenges.

Call of the Wild #F20925 by Kathy Goff for Northcott

COMPANION PANELS

Just when we think we've got this concept of working with panels figured out, along comes something new and the possibilities expand even further! Now there are companion panels!

What are companion panels? There may be 2 solo or multi-frame panels with the same theme that work together, or there may be a solo panel that has a companion panel with multiple images or frames.

If you find a set of companion panels, dive in and really let your imagination go wild!

Take a look at these whimsical 2-panel quilts, *All You Need is Love and a Dog* and *Let It Snow*.

All You Need is Love and a Dog #9051P, 24″ Dog Block
by Beth Logan for Henry Glass

All You Need is Love and a Dog #9048, 23˝ Panel by Beth Logan for Henry Glass

All You Need is Love and a Dog, 43˝ × 64˝, by Inge Ford, 2021

Inge comments, "The panels used in this quilt were bright, colorful, and appealing, but I was uncertain how to use them effectively. With the skills learned in Cyndi's workshop, along with her guidance and encouragement, I was able to find a creative way to use these two panels."

Snow Place Like Home #F5715P, companion panel for Studio E Fabrics

Snow Place Like Home #F5714, companion panel for Studio E Fabrics

Let It Snow, 60˝ × 68˝, by the author, 2021

This is my playdate with a solo snowman and a companion panel of smaller characters.
This warm and friendly flannel quilt will be great to snuggle under on cold winter evenings!

It doesn't matter which type of panel you decide to work with, the principles and ideas apply to all of them. So grab a panel and a sketch book and let's get started!

Chapter 2

Begin with the End in Mind

"Begin with the end in mind" is one of my favorite quotes from The 7 Habits of Highly Effective People *by Stephen R. Covey. I've learned from personal experience that if I don't have at least some idea of where I am going when I start working with a panel, the project or quilt can get out of hand quite quickly and unexpectedly. The project or quilt can become larger than you have space for, or the panel can become lost in the mix of fabrics, borders, and fillers you add.*

So, begin with the end in mind!

Start Planning

What were you thinking when you purchased that panel? Did you buy it with a special person or use in mind, or did you buy it just because you liked it and thought you'd figure it out later? Well, later is today … right now!

Ask yourself …

• Who is it for? Are you planning a quilt for your granddaughter, your son who is going off to college in the fall, a gift for a friend, a comfort quilt for a charity, a special wallhanging for your significant other's office wall, a table runner and placemats for a special gathering?

• How or where will it be used?

• Does it need to be a specific size or shape?

What happens if your panel is vertical, but you need it to be in a horizontal format? What if the space you have for that wall quilt is very limited? What if the panel pieces seem too big for the space or you know there is no way to use them all in one project?

If I am working with a vertical panel and my space is more horizontal, this leads me to design more on the sides of the panel and in a more asymmetrical format. Instead of adding the same size borders or blocks on all sides, I lean toward adding larger elements or blocks to the sides of the panel and narrower, smaller elements to the top and bottom.

If your wall space is limited, the opportunity to be creative using fewer fillers becomes the challenge. Perhaps only adding an interesting treatment to two sides of your panel will result in a great piece.

If your panel pieces are large or there is something that really doesn't fit your design, there are no rules that say you have to use everything! You can leave elements out, create a second piece, or put extra sections on the back.

All are great questions, and each deserves consideration as you embark on the design process. So … begin with the end in mind.

Once you know where you are going, take stock of what you know.

1. Measure the panel if it's a solo panel, or measure the size of the frames in multiple-frame panels. How many large and small elements do you have?

2. Measure the wall space, if it's going to be a wallhanging; the length of the table, if it's going to be a table runner; the size of the bed, if it's going to be a bed quilt—know your intended space.

I place my solo panel on my design wall and get a feel for if the panel is going to get lost or possibly overwhelm the space I have to work within. Use painter's tape on the design wall to outline the planned finished size of the quilt, if you have space for that, or place the solo panel in the middle of a bed or on the wall where it will ultimately live. Understanding your intended space is important, so you know if your panel is in good proportion to the space available. Your goal is to creatively fill the spaces around your panel or between the elements of the panel.

Chapter 3

Finding Design Inspiration

This is my favorite part of the process of designing and creating a panel quilt. I love exploring and discovering the possibilities a panel presents.

It helps to know where I am going (see Begin With the End in Mind, page 14), but once that is determined, then I like to live with the panel for a bit. I usually hang my panel where I can see it frequently—either on my design wall or someplace where it is really visible.

TIP • Brainstorming

I tack a sheet of scrap paper on my design wall and jot notes and ideas for several days before I begin designing, graphing, cutting, and sewing. Make notes about what you really love about this panel or who the finished project is for and what you want this quilt to say.

- Why do I like this panel?
- What attracted me to it in the beginning?
- What themes do I see within the panel? Are there flowers or hearts, or …
- What elements are there that I can highlight or emphasize?
- Are there elements in the panel that remind me of specific quilt blocks or borders?
- Is it whimsical or serious in nature? Or more geometric or organic?

Answering all of these questions can take me a long way toward creating my final design.

This will assist you as you seek design inspiration.

Example #1

Owl panel by Desiree's Designs for Quilting Treasures

I found this cute little owl panel some years ago and knew that I wanted to create a bright, cheerful baby quilt that would stimulate and capture the baby's attention—beginning with the end in mind (page 17).

The panel is fairly large for a baby quilt, so it didn't leave me much space to add borders without trimming it down. I had already decided I did not want to do that—I liked the panel as it was and, in particular, had already decided to keep the narrow bright blue frame around the panel.

As I studied the panel there were quite a few options for border design ideas:

- Leaves
- Stripes
- Polka dots
- Flowers
- Grasses
- Owls
- Tree branches
- Little colored lines within the owls themselves
- And great colors!

Lots of options! I could make a piano-key border, maybe something with stripes, circles, or grasses. I could make flower blocks or appliqué a border of flowers and leaves. I might find a patchwork block that emphasized some elements within the panel. Wow! The possibilities were endless, but what I especially liked about this panel were the little dashed lines on the owls themselves.

At the time, a number of quilters were experimenting with slashing blocks and placing fun, very thin offset strips into them. I had always wanted to try this technique and this presented the perfect opportunity. I grabbed as many fabrics as I had from my stash that included colors found in the central panel. From there, I began slashing and slicing to create blocks that added interest and created a sense of motion around the quilt.

The end result was a simple design, but a fun and stimulating border treatment that met my goal of a happy quilt that would arouse a baby's curiosity.

Owl Family, 34˝ × 49˝, by the author, 2017

Example #2

Over the past few years, Hoffman California Fabrics has been creating beautiful panels featuring wildlife. The panels vary in size, but most of them are large enough to showcase on a bed quilt or turn into a stunning wall quilt. When I work with these panels, I like to really study and discover the elements.

This panel of a bear became a striking wall quilt when Connie Anderson carefully focused on the themes and elements within the panel and highlighted the colors to enhance her design. Connie kept the panel as a central medallion in her wall quilt and concentrated on what she could see, both literally and figuratively.

The bear was traveling forward, so Connie found a drawing of some bear footprints and appliquéd those onto a beautifully textured brown fabric in the area below the panel. The texture of the fabric gave the illusion of dirt.

Inspired by the soft images of pine trees on the back of the bear, she created appliquéd trees and placed them near the footprints.

On the sides of the panel, Connie wanted to give the illusion of snowflakes, so she chose pinwheel blocks in subtle colors to provide the sense of movement of the flakes in the winter sky. In the upper corners, she placed traditional Bear Paw quilt blocks and added a row of Flying Geese blocks along the top of the panel. Finally, she added a checkerboard top border to complete the composition. The result is an exquisite piece of quilted artwork.

The Alaskan Bear, 42˝ × 55˝, by Connie Anderson, 2020

Connie says, "I named this quilt after I saw this wonderful panel hanging in a quaint little quilt shop in Skagway, Alaska. I used elements from the panel, such as the geese, trees, and bear paws to enhance the majesty of the bear."

Example #3

One last example—because sometimes we just want to have fun!

I tell my students that just because it's a fabric panel and you might be a quilt maker, does not mean that every panel has to end up in a standard-shaped quilt! There are lots of ways to use panels, and this was one of my favorite "play" projects.

The original panel included 8 whimsical Christmas-themed characters and a row of little snowflakes. I wanted to get out of the "it's got to be a quilt" box with this one, so I decided to create a table runner for my holiday table.

Panel by Victoria Hutto for Quilting Treasures

Holiday table runner, 24˝ × 51˝, by the author, 2018

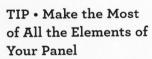

TIP • Make the Most of All the Elements of Your Panel

Panels often have a border along one side or small elements that you can save and incorporate into some part of your design. Don't discard them—try to find a way to use them creatively!

I chose to use only 4 of the characters and decided that since the table runner would lay flat on a table rather than hang on a wall, I would alternate the orientation of the characters. Guests on either side of the table would have "company" during dinner!

I set the character pieces with rows of simple patchwork squares between them and then added small 4˝ patchwork blocks above each character, for interest. Notice that I found a way to use those little snowflakes in the center of some of those patchwork blocks.

I added a red frame around this central part of my table runner and then added a floating checkerboard border, off-set with small Sawtooth Star blocks, where I again used those small snowflakes from the panel as part of the design.

I didn't stop here though—I wanted more fun on my table, so back to the quilt shop I went to pick up another of these panels. I decided placemats would make a great addition to my table runner. I kept those pretty simple, using some improvisational log-cabin-style piecing to frame the characters, and once again fitting those snowflakes in somewhere on every placemat.

Once the placemats were complete, I discovered I had 4 pieces I hadn't used so … I made potholders!

Panels need not be limited to quilts or wallhangings. Make a bag to carry books to class, trick or treat bags for your grandkids, pillows for your bedroom, coasters … the possibilities are endless, if you let your imagination run free!

Class Project bag,
by the author, 2018

Pretty Little Things
panel by Louise Allen
for Wilmington Prints

TIP • Appliqué Motifs

When I choose to create appliqué motifs for my panel quilts, I will often photocopy sections of the panel itself (for personal use), then enlarge or reduce them to the desired sizes to create patterns that complement the overall theme of my panel project. If I need something like paw prints or other elements, Google Images has tons of line drawings and free graphics for personal use.

Chapter 4

Dealing with "Wonky" Panels and Odd-Sized Sections

Help! This panel is crooked ... these measurements are weird ... what should I do?

Let's face it, working with panels comes with its own set of unique challenges. Panels can have odd measurements, be printed askew, or the frames in a set aren't all the same size. These challenges often cause us to fold the panel up and return it to the fabric cupboard. But don't give up just yet!

Wash Your Panel

If your panel is a bit wonky, start by machine washing and drying the panel because sometimes the chemicals applied to the fabric and the process of winding the fabric onto bolts can cause distortions that can be easily and simply remedied. I always prewash, dry, and block or press my panels before I use them.

PRESSING

If washing and drying your panel doesn't solve the problem, and your panel is still slightly wonky, pressing the panel with steam and squirting it with water in a spray bottle can make a big difference. I like to press a little, check my progress with my large square rulers, press again and repeat the process until my piece is as square as possible. Ultimately, you'll have to commit to one corner or edge of the panel or frame as being square and progress from that spot. Once I have it right where I want it, I apply some spray starch or other starch product, lightly press, then place my square ruler on top of the panel to confirm it is still square, add some books on top, and let it dry. Sometimes this process feels a bit like wrestling, but it's worth the effort.

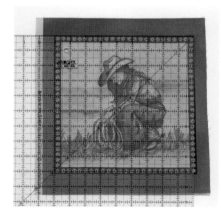

Pressing pieces to square them

Blocking

If your panel is quite wonky, try blocking it. I draw lines vertically and horizontally at 90° angles on large stabilizer sheets, which I pin to my design wall, so I have reference points. I wash the panel, and before it is fully dry, I pin it to my design wall about every 2˝ to 3˝ across the entire panel, smoothing and aligning as I go. Then, I let it dry completely. Once it is dry on the blocking sheet, I'll press it using a bit of starch to help the piece maintain its new shape while I sew it into my project.

The first question I get that follows the above description is, "Won't the panel go back to its original shape?" My answer is, not likely. If you have washed the fabric, added starch, pressed, allowed to dry, or blocked the panel, it isn't inclined to return to its previous form. Once you have sewn it into your well-planned and executed piece, it's not going anywhere.

Odd-Sized Sections

Okay, that all sounds great, but what happens when the panel has some strange measurements?

First, you have to decide which elements from your panel you want to use and which ones to save for another project.

Solo panels sometimes have one or more printed frames around them, and you may wish to keep the frame as a border or eliminate them. Ask yourself if the frame enhances the panel or could be discarded. If you keep it, you might encounter some challenging math, but we will deal with that in the next section on adding coping strips. If you eliminate those frames or make them narrower, you can trim the panel to a measurement that you are comfortable working with. Don't forget to add seam allowance when you trim your panels!

Blocking a full panel

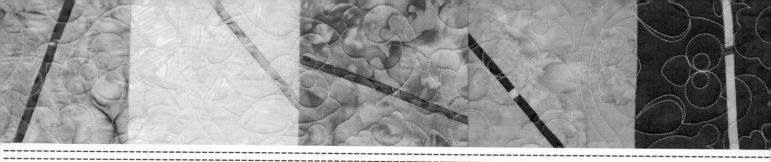

Adding Coping Strips

If you need your panel or block to be a specific size, you might need to add vertical and/or horizontal pieces of fabric on some or all of the edges to make them the desired size you will need for your project. I call these "coping strips." Some of my students call them "fudging strips." Coping strips are different from borders in that they serve a very definite purpose—getting you from the size you have to the size you want. This allows you to deal with crazy measurements, so you can move forward with your design.

Note: Before you cut the actual panel, remember to add the ¼˝ seam allowance to *all* four edges.

Let's work through the following quilt example together. This panel had a narrow blue frame and a narrow black frame. I had to determine if I wanted to keep one, both, or neither of these narrow frames. I chose to keep the blue frame in the finished quilt because I liked the way it framed the panel and highlighted the darker blue color.

In the quilt, I chose to add a border of pieced blocks on all sides of the center panel. Before I could begin adding the pieced-block border, however, I had to determine what size blocks would work best. In order to do this, I had to add coping strips to the center panel.

Owl Family; the orange borders are the coping strips.

VERTICAL (SIDE EDGES) COPING STRIPS

The *unfinished* panel width measured 22″ from the outer edges of the blue printed frames. The *finished* width, including the blue frame but not the seam allowance, is 21½″.

This 21½″ measurement does not divide into a whole number evenly and since I wanted to keep that blue frame as a border, I determined that the next number easily divided by a whole number is 25. So, 5″ blocks it is!

Now, 25″ is where I want to be and 21½″ is where I am.

25″ minus 21½″ equals 3½″ of coping strips that need to be added to make the panel 25″ wide.

Since I want to keep the panel symmetrical, I want equal-width coping strips on each vertical side edge of the panel. Dividing 3½″ by 2 equals 1¾″. I will need to add a 1¾″ coping strip to each side of the panel. **Remember, none of this math includes seam allowance! Don't cut yet!**

Add ½″ to the 1¾″ coping strip width to equal 2¼″ to include the ¼″ seam allowance on each side of the strip. You will need 2 strips this width.

Cut 2 strips 2¼″ wide × the fabric width selvage to selvage. Measure and cut the correct length for the strips; in this case, the length of the panel.

‖ **NOTE** *Do not just add a long strip and cut it off at the bottom—this will result in stretching and distortion.*

Sew the strips to the side edges of the panel. Press.

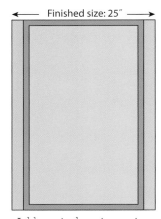

When sewn to the sides, the *unfinished* width of the panel will be 25½″. The *finished* width will be 25″, which divides quite nicely by 5″ finished blocks!

Add vertical coping strips.

HORIZONTAL (TOP AND BOTTOM EDGES) COPING STRIPS

Now for the length of my piece: The unfinished panel measured 35½″ from the outer edges of the top and bottom blue printed frames. The finished length of this panel, including the blue frame but not the seam allowance, is 35″. That does divide by 5″ (the size of the blocks I wanted to use), but I thought it might look a bit odd if I only added coping strips to the sides, so I chose to add coping strips to the top and bottom edges as well.

Following the same process, I need to get to the next number that is divisible by 5 which is 40.

The difference between where I want to go (40″) and where I am (35″) is 5″.

If I plan an equal-width coping strip at both the top and bottom edges of the panel, I need 2½″ for each.

Add ½″ to the 2½″ coping strip width to equal 3″ to include the ¼″ seam allowance on each side of the strip. You will need 2 strips this width.

Cut 2 strips 3″ wide × the fabric width selvage to selvage. Measure and cut the correct measurement for the strips; in this case, the measurement is 25½″, which includes seam allowance.

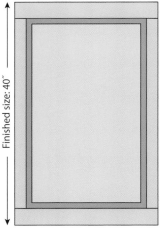

How coping strips get you from where you are to where you need to be!

Coping strips can serve you well in almost every panel type. If you have multiple frames that have odd measurements, treat them in exactly the same fashion—they're just smaller! If you have very small frames from panels that you want to work into traditional quilt blocks and you can't cut them to fit because they are too small, try adding coping strips!

Chapter 5

Discover the Magic in Traditional Quilt Blocks

Learning to work with solo panels means learning about things like the scale and proportion of the patchwork you add around the central panel. Be sure to audition your ideas either on graph paper or on a design wall before you start cutting! For instance, if your panel is X inches wide by Y inches long, what are your options for how many blocks of various sizes can be placed on the horizontal and vertical sides of your panel, and which sizes look best?

Using traditional quilt blocks to feature the same-sized frames of panels or to use as filler between motifs and panel sections is a wonderful design element, and knowing how to graph them to the space you need to fill is essential!

When determining if a traditional block might be used to highlight a section of a panel, I look for open space—or where I can create open space—within the block. Depending on the size of the panel element and how big you want to make a particular block, it can be the perfect place to highlight some panel elements.

For example, the Sawtooth Star block has a fantastic open space in the center which is fairly large. Look for quilt blocks that already have space or where you can leave out portions to create this space.

I used this block in my table runner in both the border and body of the piece and as a 14˝ block in my quilt *Dog Stars* (page 31).

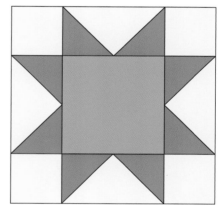

Detail from *Dog Stars* quilt
(See photo of full quilt, page 31.)

Detail from *Holiday* table runner (See photo of full runner, page 19.)

Below is another example of using elements from the panel in traditional quilt blocks. It shows how both larger and smaller elements from the panel were incorporated into 2 quilt blocks to create this winter-themed wall quilt. This panel included four different small animals and one larger deer.

Winter Wildlife Star, 42˝ × 42˝, by the author, 2020

Notice where Jean Weller used elements of her panel inside Log Cabin and Ohio Star blocks in her quilt (below)!

Shore Birds, 72˝ × 80˝, by Jean Pridham Weller, quilted by Trudy Dey, 2020

Jean writes, "I am a bird photographer and spend most winters in Texas, photographing birds. The Shore Bird Collection panel reminded me of my wonderful times photographing these birds. When designing the quilt, I needed more bird blocks, so I made Ohio Stars with flying seagulls in the center. Log Cabin strips surround each bird and are arranged so they form a zig zag pattern. A strip with half-square triangles was added to the top and bottom to make the quilt rectangular instead of square. A piano key border adds interest to the quilt."

Another unique way to use traditional quilt blocks to both highlight sections of the panel or create an appealing twist is to create a row-by-row quilt with a panel (or two), especially those with same-sized elements. In *Horses Are My Joy!* (below), my focus was to find blocks that emphasized themes from the panel and used frames from the panel within the row-by-row quilt.

Horses Are My Joy!, 61″ × 74″, by the author, 2021

My daughter and I share a love of horses. This quilt was designed to commemorate
the love of those we've lost and those who still capture our hearts.

Notice my quilt where I inserted 7˝ elements from this whimsical dog panel into six different traditional star quilt blocks.

Dog Stars, 60˝ × 72˝, by the author, 2017

In creating this quilt, I discovered how to square up individual panel sections. The quilt is a play on words as some of the dogs are featured in the centers of star blocks and I am fascinated by Dog Stars in the night sky.

Play, have fun, try things—you'll find just what will work best for showcasing parts of your panel! Here's a collection of traditional blocks to consider including in your quilt. They all have open space in which to insert a panel segment; some blocks have been altered to create more space for larger segments.

3 × 3 Blocks

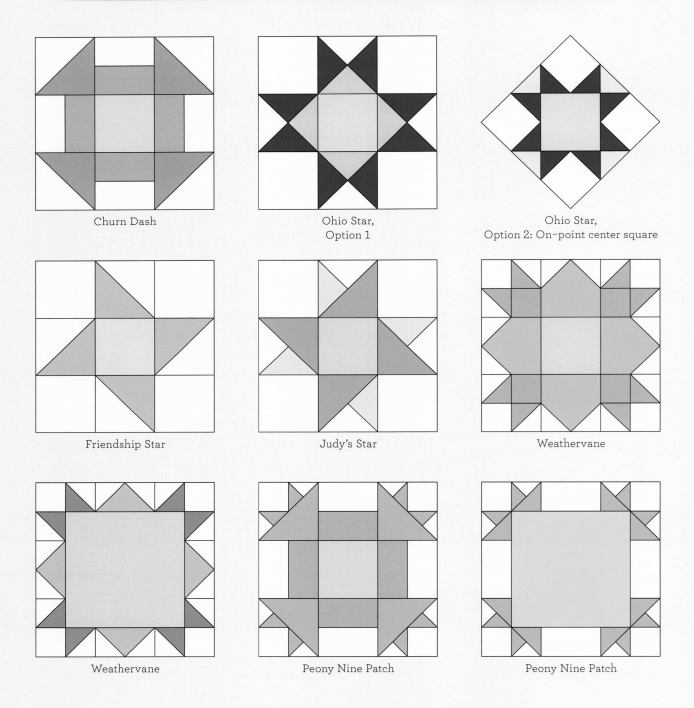

Churn Dash

Ohio Star,
Option 1

Ohio Star,
Option 2: On-point center square

Friendship Star

Judy's Star

Weathervane

Weathervane

Peony Nine Patch

Peony Nine Patch

Mother's Choice,
Option 1

Mother's Choice,
Option 2: On-point center square

Mother's Choice,
Option 3

Kings Crown Variation,
Option 1: On-point center square

Kings Crown Variation,
Option 2

Sister's Choice,
Option 1

Sister's Choice,
Option 2: On-point center square

Sister's Choice,
Option 3

Puss in the Corner,
Option 1

Puss in the Corner,
Option 2

Puss in the Corner,
Option 3

4 × 4 Blocks

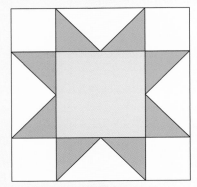

Sawtooth Star,
Option 1

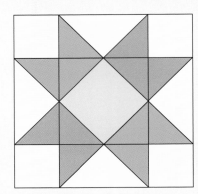

Sawtooth Star,
Option 2: This variation offers a
smaller center.

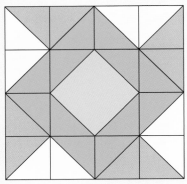

Windblown,
Option 1

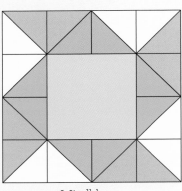

Windblown,
Option 2

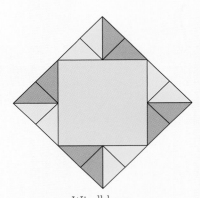

Windblown,
Option 3: On-point center square

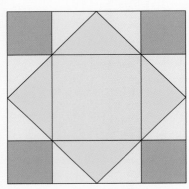

Union variation,
Option 1

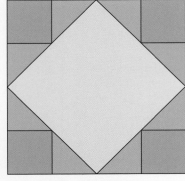

Union variation,
Option 2

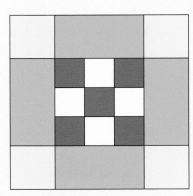

Honey Bee Variation 1

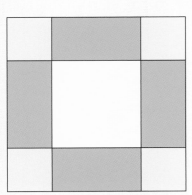

Honey Bee Variation 2

Storm at Sea,
Option 1

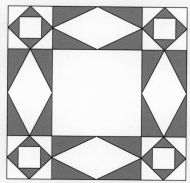

Storm at Sea,
Option 2

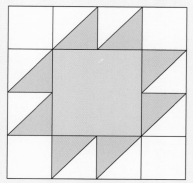

Anvil: Replace the 4 small center
squares with 1 larger square.

Great Miscellaneous Options

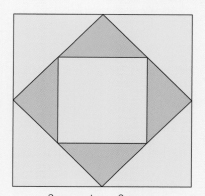

Square-in-a-Square,
Option 1

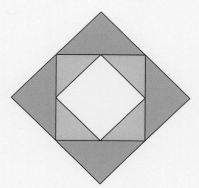

Square-in-a-Square,
Option 2

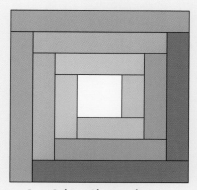

Log Cabin: Change the size
of the center square and use as many
or as few logs as you want.

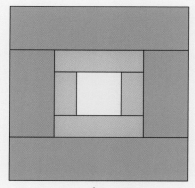

Framed Squares

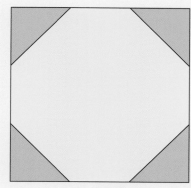

Snowball

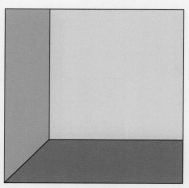

Attic Window

Graphing

A graph is a simple diagram drawn on gridded paper that allows you to lay out your block and quilts designs, determine the exact measurements of all the elements of your quilt, and avoid bloopers and mistakes! It shows the relationship of your elements or pieces to each other, helps you make everything the right size so it all fits nicely into your quilt, and simplifies your sewing. The easiest, most accurate way to graph (or lay out) your quilt is to use graph paper.

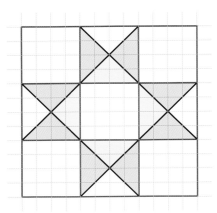

> **TIP • Helpful Tools**
>
> My favorite graph paper is Graph-It Quilt Design Graph Paper by June Tailor. This 12″ × 12″ graph paper is perfect because quilt blocks are typically square. And it is subdivided into 4 small squares per inch. The standard 8½″ × 11″ graph paper will also work fine, but be sure the paper is subdivided 4 to the inch and not 5 or 10. I use an office ruler or school ruler, a mechanical pencil, and Erasable Colored Pencils by Crayola. These are the tools I find most helpful when I am starting to get my design down on paper.

Graphing by hand is much easier than it sounds. Of course, if you have a computer program, you can use this instead.

To begin, a basic understanding and ability to recognize the grid that a quilt block is based on is essential. For a more detailed understanding of graphing, check out *Drafting for the Creative Quilter* by Sally Collins (C&T Publishing).

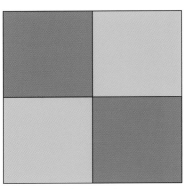

2 × 2 grid

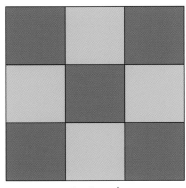

3 × 3 grid

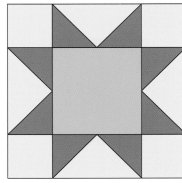

4 × 4 grid

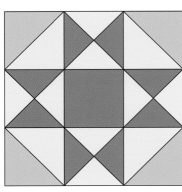

3 × 3 grid

Why is it important to understand the grid you are working within when working with panels? I like to incorporate some of the smaller elements often found in panels into my traditional quilt blocks. Take a look at the following examples.

3 × 3 grid; I used a section of the panel in the center of this Rose Star block (see *It's All About the Girl* quilt, page 44).

4 × 4 grid; see how the large deer fits nicely into this block from my *Winter Wonderland* quilt (page 57).

Knowing how to graph and incorporate bits of your panel into existing quilt blocks offers you endless design possibilities, so practice using a few of these basic blocks and seeing what different sizes you can graph them. The Sawtooth Star block in the *Holiday* table runner and *Dog Stars* quilt (pages 19 and 31) is a wonderful block that can easily be graphed and used as a 4˝, 6˝, 8˝, 10˝, or 12˝ block and is a good one to practice with.

TIP • Graph in Finished Sizes
Remember when graphing that you are working with *finished sizes*. Be sure to add seam allowances to the pieces when you cut them.

Chapter 6

Working from a Map or Grid

Before going forward, you need a basic plan. How are you going to use your center panel or framed motifs? Are you going to add blocks or Flying Geese or a checkerboard around the panel? Are you going to have a border with detailed appliqué that requires some spatial planning? No matter what comes next, before you get started, create a grid drawing of your quilt to use as your map.

TIP • Use an Ounce of Caution

It's easy to get carried away either through the use of too many busy fabrics or too many competing elements, so strive for unity and harmony in your project.

Try this: Cut out the elements of your panel leaving as much border around the printed designs as possible. Begin by arranging them on your design wall in a pleasing fashion. This can apply to a panel with same-sized frames or a panel with frames of varying sizes. Play with the layout, move them around, add more, or leave some out.

TIPS

• An option to cutting out your panel motifs is to color photocopy the elements of your panel at full size (except the center solo panel) and arrange them on your design wall. Then, you can cut up your panel after you have a solid plan.

• Remember to leave space around the elements for seam allowance or blocking as you cut.

Once you have arranged the panel elements where you like them, the next step is to craft some kind of map or grid.

I often loosely sketch the design on plain paper first and begin doodling what I might want to put between

the panel segments. This gives me some idea of where I want to go. Perhaps I want to fill between sections with a row of Flying Geese, or maybe I want to use a traditional block and add part of my panel in an open space.

When I have those ideas sketched, I create a map/grid on graph paper. This step is important because you cannot simply start making Flying Geese units if they aren't actually going to fit into the particular space. Settle in with graph paper and map out where those panel pieces will land.

Another option is to cut small replicas of your panel segments from colored paper using the scale of your graph paper and your panel elements, then move them around, much like designing a room layout, until you are happy with where they live on your map before committing them to the space. This will help avoid unnecessary drawing and erasing.

TIP • The Magical Pencil Tool

One note here; you have to be a tad flexible, so don't forget that your pencil comes with 2 handy tools—the lead *and* the eraser!

Having designated where the panel pieces will go, you can then determine the sizes of the fill elements. If you want Flying Geese units, what size will they need to be to fit in that space? Do you need to move one of the panel elements just a bit to accommodate the filler? Do you want to simply add a spacer strip between the geese units or halfway across or ... ? How are you going to fill the space effectively? Sometimes I get it all graphed out and after I start making blocks or borders, I juggle things around to achieve a better flow, balance, or layout.

Remember that *flexibility* is the name of the game, so if you don't like how it's coming out on your map, change something!

I designed *Beach Day* using a panel by Blank Quilting (Shore Thing, page 9). These panel segments were rectangular instead of square, so there was an additional challenge in creating the design. My motto is "play and have fun," so I decided adding words as filler in some of the spaces might be a creative way to proceed. I also used the striped-fabric areas of the panel in the pieced fish blocks in the lower left area of the quilt.

Beach Day, 48˝ × 52˝, by the author, 2020

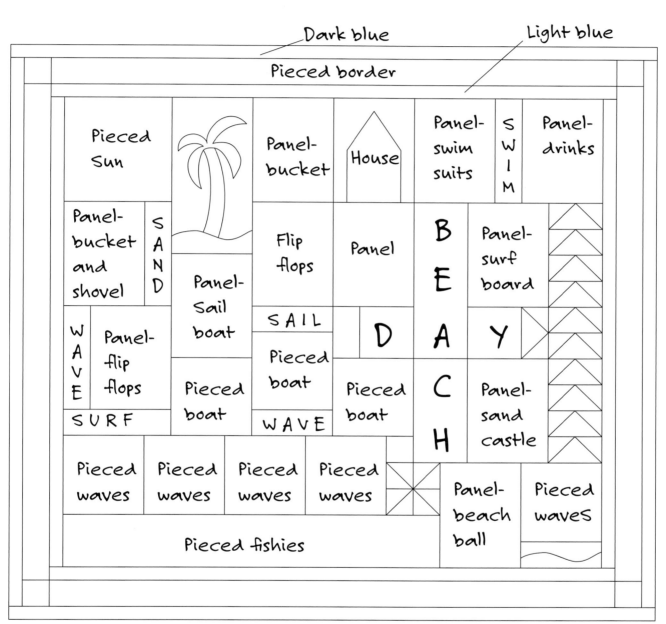

Map/grid of design for *Beach Day*

Look at the grid below for Adam S. Holladay's quilt, *Winter's First Snow*, using the Winter Cardinals panel from Hoffman Fabrics. And see the beautiful quilt on page 43 that came about after he got all of his designs on graph paper!

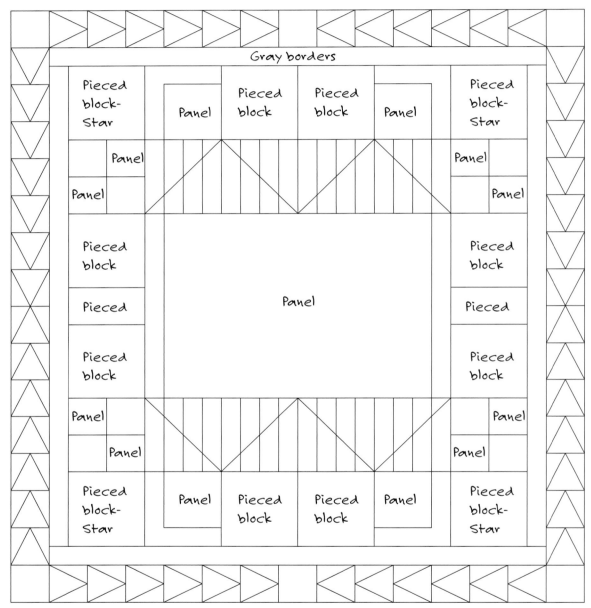

Map/grid of design for *Winter's First Snow*

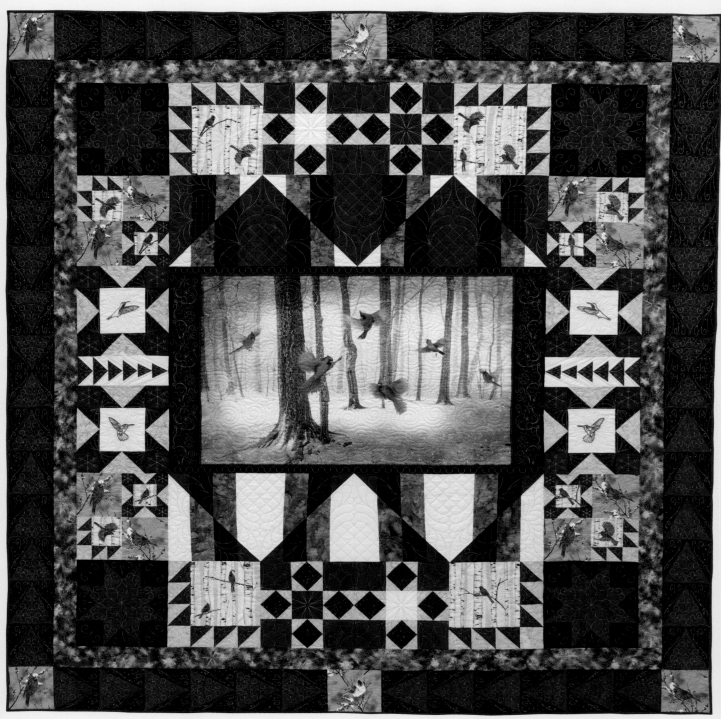

Winter's First Snow, 90˝ × 92˝, designed and pieced by Adam S. Holladay, quilted by Cyndi McChesney, 2021

Adam describes this quilt, "A winter-theme design combining a dominant color and blended neutral fabrics in support of a central panel."

Chapter 7

Gallery of Quilts

In the following pages, you'll find many wonderful examples of quilts created by me and by students who have participated in my workshops over the past few years. They are included here with permission and with some comments from the maker. Enjoy!

It's All About the Girl, 49˝ × 53˝, by the author, 2016

I created this quilt for my daughter who is a farrier. The panel caught my attention because of the section featuring the boots, spurs, and hat. I wanted that to be the focal point in this wall quilt, but also chose to feature small sections of the panel inside of traditional quilt blocks.

Friends, 40˝ × 60˝, by the author, 2017

This quilt came about because I received a gift of 60 fat quarters in reds, blacks, and grays.
I chose simple border treatments in order to use all 60 of the fat quarters.

Wildlife in the Living Room, 44˝ × 54˝, designed and constructed by Adele Drake, quilted by Cyndi McChesney, 2018

Adele tells the story behind the quilt: "My husband challenged me to make a quilt
that was more 'manly,' so this was my gift to him."

Scroll Work, table topper, 35˝ × 35˝, by Trina Jahnsen, 2021

Trina comments, "I purchased several yards of these scrollwork panels because I thought they were elegant and would make great placemats. But after taking Cyndi's class, I decided a table topper would be more creative and interesting."

Olivia the Pig, 38″ × 38″, by Cheryl Thomason-Lethco, 2021

Cheryl remembers, "Years ago I was gifted a bag of Olivia the Pig fabric and really didn't know what to do with it. On a whim I signed up for the San Juan Quilters Guild workshop on panels being taught by Cyndi McChesney (fantastic teacher!). Olivia was soon creating herself into a wallhanging. I even incorporated a couple of 3-D Bowtie blocks!"

The Sentinel, 58˝ × 70˝, by Maureen Collop, 2020

Maureen notes, "My quilt was made for my granddaughter, Emerson, who loves wolves.
She lives in Colorado, so I wanted to include mountains, starry skies, snow, and tall trees."

Hummingbird Garden, 25˝ × 27˝, by Lilla M. Hall, 2021

Lilla recalls, "Every step in designing this wallhanging unfolded in stages. Choosing the different values of the green bricks was a suggestion from Cyndi in our class. Adding the razzle dazzle meandering thread work on the poppies was a reaction to a suggestion by another quilter who thought a little bling would add interest. The trapunto behind the center poppies was my decision to add some depth to the work. The poppies on the top and bottom are tacked on to suggest movement and distance. The hand quilting on the sides, top, and bottom are imitating random flowing stems. The echo hand quilting was done to lift the large poppies in the center of the panel."

Poppies, 34˝ × 50˝, by Deborah Jenkins, 2021

From Deborah: "I love feeding the hummingbirds that visit each year; I so enjoy watching their aerobatics at the feeders and throughout the yard. I have started planting flowers to attract butterflies also, hoping to have a view like this panel in the future."

Cardinals in the Air, 33˝ × 48˝, by Nancy C. Judd, 2021

Nancy met a challenge with this quilt: "I used cardinals from a Call of the Wild series panel
by Hoffman California Fabrics. I cut the cardinals asymmetrically from the panel and placed them on a layout board.
Then, I pieced log-cabin strips joining the cardinals. I used some of the background panel fabric to fill in various spaces.
I chose to veer away from traditional patchwork and designed an improvisational piece using this panel."

Christmas Cardinals, 45″ × 51″, by Annick Harris, quilted by Nancy Judd, 2021

Annick recalls, "The original Benartex panel had gold roping and a lot of red around the individual frames in this panel.
I created a fascinating network of paths and trimmed the individual sections of the panel to work with the map
I drew for this quilt using traditional Birds in the Air and Migrating Geese to highlight the theme.
The panel and all the fabrics in this quilt had also been in my stash for a long time."

Witch Quilt Show, 42˝ × 54˝, by Beth Kendall, 2021

As noted by Beth, "I started out with a plan for this panel but discovered along the way that sometimes a panel will lead you down a different path. My friends at a quilt retreat thought I was crazy to make tiny little quilts inspired by the panel prints by the Salem Quilt Guild, but I love how it pulled the quilt together."

Home for Christmas, 48″ × 53″, by Karen Ferguson, 2021

Karen created something special with this quilt: "I really spread my wings on this quilt, creating a house completely on my own with lots of intricate piecing and detail! The red truck reminded me of a truck we had on our farm when I was a child. We called the truck Ida Red. My dad bought it brand new and I will never forget that 'new' smell!"

To Be or Not To Be, 38˝ × 45˝, by Vi Koch, 2020

Vi comments, "The little animals on this panel and the selvage blocks complement each other.
This keeps the viewer's eye moving around the quilt."

Winter Wonderland, 90″ × 90″, by Tammy Hamel, 2020

Tammy says, "I chose to highlight my panel segments simply by alternating them with an interesting patchwork quilt block. I thoroughly enjoyed a trunk show provided to my quilt guild by Cyndi McChesney. It was all about creative ways to do a panel quilt. I missed the class the next day, but Cyndi's input gave me the inspiration to start this project that I'd had the panels and fabric for at least 3 years. I look forward to making my next panel quilt!"

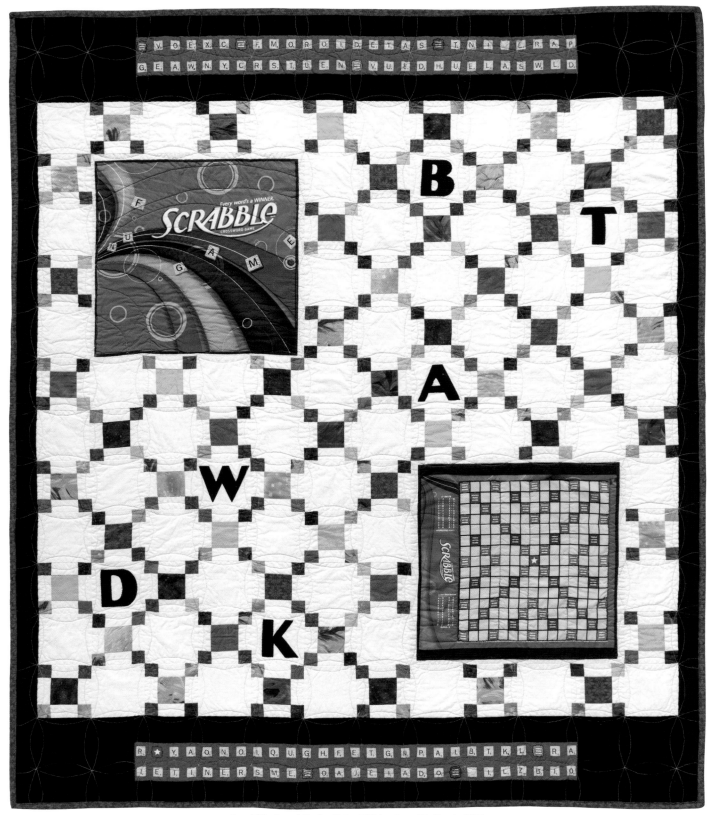

Scrabble Panel Quilt, 49˝ × 58˝, by Joan Holland, 2020

Joan remembers, "I purchased this panel about four years ago with the idea of making a travel game. I was a novice so it didn't happen. My guild offered the Panel Palooza workshop, which gave me the opportunity to learn about possibilities from an experienced teacher plus share ideas with the other participants, and I am thrilled with the outcome."

The Three Tenors, 66˝ × 73˝, by Carole Dehlinger

Panel by Penny Rose Studio; the wolves are appliquéd onto a background of Typospheres fabric by Lonni Rossi.

Window Garden, 30˝ × 40˝, by Sandra L. Smith

Sandra noted about this quilt, "I did *not* want to cut this panel apart, but Cyndi finally persuaded me.
I knew that I wanted the bottles of flowers sitting on a windowsill, and I love appliqué over pieced backgrounds,
so I pieced the sky that is seen through the window. The top of the window was looking naked, so I decided
to create a stained-glass transom effect. I raw-edge appliquéd the flower bottles."

Blue Santa, 74″ × 74″, by the author, 2012

Blue Santa was one of the earliest quilts from panels I created, and I include it here as a bit of a cautionary tale!
Be careful not to let your borders and your excitement carry you away. The outer borders are, perhaps, a bit too big
for the small central panel. I was having fun and learning as I went, so remember to begin with the end in mind!

Chapter 8

Helpful Resources

Finding Appliqué Motifs

If you've chosen to use appliqué and feel you can't draw to save your life, where can you find appliqué motifs?

The panel itself is a super resource for appliqué motifs. If there is a particular element such as a flower, a tree, or a heart that I want to use in my quilt as an appliqué design, I take my panel to my printer and photocopy the fabric. It's easy to enlarge or reduce these elements, either on your own printer or at your local copy shop.

If the motif you want isn't easy to photocopy, Google Images is a great tool for finding non-copyrighted images. You can simply type in what you are looking for or search using the words "line drawing." Results will yield dozens of images that you can turn into appliqué patterns. You can size any image up or down from your print format page or on a copier.

Coloring books are another wonderful source of appliqué motifs with simple, clean lines, and children's and adult's books yield lots of designs that make great appliqué motifs.

> **NOTE** *Unless it's specifically noted that these designs are copyright free, designs that were not designed by you should not be used for commercial purposes.*

Quilt Block Ideas

What about quilt blocks or quilt block elements in varieties of sizes? Once again, you can simply search on Google Images and then graph the blocks yourself, now that you know how! If you're not quite sure what you're looking for or prefer a paper-pieced block, check out Quilter's Cache (quilterscache.com) and Generations Quilt Patterns (generations-quilt-patterns.com). There are literally hundreds of blocks on these sites and they are available in a wide range of sizes. Even better, most are *free!*

The following are must-haves for your quilting library:

Encyclopedia of Pieced Quilt Patterns by Barbara Brackman (Electric Quilt)

The Skill-Building Quick & Easy Block Tool (C&T Publishing) with 110 blocks in five sizes

There are many wonderful books full of quilt blocks and borders—ask your local quilt shop to offer some of these or to special order one you find online. Your local library has shelves of books covering everything from early primitive art to the intricate scrolls of the Renaissance to our modern, graphic art. Sometimes a small section of something larger is exactly what you need!

Look through those magazines you've been saving, books already in your personal library, and the patterns you have in your studio. You'll find lots of great examples and maybe even some unique options to add to your quilt.

More Learning Resources

If you'd like to delve more deeply into elements of design, I highly recommend adding *Adventures in Design* by Joen Wolfrom (C&T Publishing), to your personal library. This book is a fantastic resource.

Another terrific program of study is presented on The Quilt Show (thequiltshow.com) with Lilo Bowman. You'll want to become a member and watch every lesson!

Having fun graphing or want to learn more? A must-have book is, *Drafting for the Creative Quilter* by Sally Collins (C&T Publishing).

About the Author

Upon graduation from college in 1978, the first thing Cyndi did was to enroll in a beginning quiltmaking class, and she quickly became immersed in all things quilt related! Through this book, Cyndi hopes to challenge and encourage quilters while inspiring confidence to discover their own innate creativity in the design and construction of unique projects from the many wonderful pre-printed panels available today.

As a National Quilt Association Certified Teacher of the Year, Cyndi has enjoyed teaching throughout the US and Canada and is known for her humorous and detailed teaching expertise.

Cyndi operates her longarm quilting business from her home studio in northwest Arkansas and has won awards in shows such as the Hoffman Challenge, Mancuso Visuals #1, the Vermont Quilt Festival, and many more. When not pursuing creative endeavors, she enjoys road cycling trips, walking her dog, reading, and traveling. Join Cyndi in 2023 for a quilt-related tour to The Netherlands and Belgium!

Correspondence may be sent directly to Cyndi via email at cyndimcchesney@gmail.com.

Visit Cyndi online and follow on social media!

Website: cedarridgequilting.com · **Facebook:** /cedarridgequilting